S. L.-Görg

Aspects of Race and Parallels with the "Third Reich" in J.K. Rowling's "Harry Potter and the Order of the Phoenix"

GRIN Publishing

Bibliographic information published by the German National Library:

The German National Library lists this publication in the National Bibliography; detailed bibliographic data are available on the Internet at http://dnb.dnb.de .

Imprint:

Copyright © 2014 GRIN Verlag, Open Publishing GmbH
Print and binding: Books on Demand GmbH, Norderstedt Germany
ISBN: 978-3-668-00428-3

This book at GRIN:

http://www.grin.com/en/e-book/301147/aspects-of-race-and-parallels-with-the-third-reich-in-j-k-rowling-s

GRIN - Your knowledge has value

Since its foundation in 1998, GRIN has specialized in publishing academic texts by students, college teachers and other academics as e-book and printed book. The website www.grin.com is an ideal platform for presenting term papers, final papers, scientific essays, dissertations and specialist books.

Institut für Anglistik und
Amerikanistik

Wintersemester 2013/2014

Bachelorarbeit

Aspects of race and parallels with the *Third Reich* in J.K. Rowling's
Harry Potter and the Order of the Phoenix

Ba/Ma Lehramt im Modellversuch 2005, BfP
Anglistik und Amerikanistik FS: 9
Rehabilitationspädagogik FS: 7

Content

1. Introduction

Although 'Pottermania', as the newspapers have called the huge hype around Joanne K. Rowling's *Harry Potter* books, has come to an end, the *Harry Potter* series can still be seen as the most influential and most popular fantasy novels of our time. Children and adults around the world have read the stories of how the adolescent wizard Harry and his friends Ron and Hermione fight against Lord Voldemort and his followers. Professors of the Anglistik and Amerikanistik, such as Prof. Dr. Kullmann even claim that *Harry Potter* has the potential to become a classic and can be mentioned in the same breath with *Alice in Wonderland* or *The Hobbit* (DieWelt2012). Despite all the praise for the novels, also many critics have reflected about and commented on J.K. Rowling's novels.

In my bachelor thesis I am going to take a more critical look at the *Harry Potter* series, focusing mainly on Rowling's fifth novel titled *Harry Potter and the Order of the Phoenix*, which builds the basis of my text oriented analysis.

As the title of my bachelor thesis: *Aspects of race and parallels with the Third Reich in J.K. Rowling's Harry Potter and the Order of the Phoenix* already reveals, I will examine the novel in terms of its hidden parallels towards the beliefs and practices in the *Third Reich* as well as the aspects of race and racism which become obvious while analyzing the novel.

Before defining the aspect of race and racism and applying it to the beliefs of Adolf Hitler and to the ideas conveyed in *Harry Potter* in the first part of my paper, I will shortly point out why children's fantasy books are worth analyzing, what kind of a fantasy novel *Harry Potter* is, and which approaches I used for my analysis.

The second part of my thesis is going to focus on the parallels between the *Third Reich* and the world presented in *Harry Potter and the Order of the Phoenix*. My focus here is going to be on political changes, such as the infiltration of the school system or the establishment of new laws made during this specific period of time as well as on the

3

consequences these changes had for society. Finally I will point out how it was possible to fight against and finally beat the Lord Voldemort by taking a closer look at underground movements such as the *Order of the Phoenix* and *Dumbledore's Army*.

2. *Harry Potter* as Fantasy Novel

Before starting to analyze Joanne K. Rowling's *Harry Potter* series, it is essential to point out the relevance of children's books and to define to which kind of fantasy novel *Harry Potter* belongs. Furthermore it will be pointed out why a children's fantasy novel is important in order to understand culture.

First of all, children's books are by no means trivial, but "powerful literature" (Hunt 1) which is valuable to analyze because "it is a cultural and ideological construct explicitly or implicitly transporting adults notions of social, ethnic, cultural, gender and literary-aesthetic norms" (Bimberg 321). In detail this means that children's literature is a "debased form of an adult text" (Hunt 4) that often depicts the same cultural and social problems adults have, but transfer it to a different level for the child reader. Besides, children's literature offers not only "links with literary and cultural studies" but also with "history, politics, sociology psychology, psychotherapy and pedagogics" (Bimberg 322). Consequently, children's books such as *Harry Potter* can be called a cross-cultural and interdisciplinary work that is important to analyze due to the hidden parallels to the adult world and to the criticism which is "closely associated with general/adult literature, culture, theory and criticism" (Lesnik- Oberstein 25; 27).

Concerning the classification of *Harry Potter* within the field of fantasy literature, one first of all has to note that fantasy is a genre that is "resistant to attempts at quick definition" (Grenby 144) because even the broadest attempt to define fantasy as "fiction involving the supernatural or impossible" (Manlove 3) bears complications. Difficulties might arise because the supernatural as well as "the impossible and the unreal are not fixed" (Grenby 145). For example as time goes by, capabilities of what people can do, change. Stories that might have been considered fantasy stories in the past, because they for instance involved flights to the outer space, can no longer be called fantasy stories because for astronauts, flying to the outer space is now taking place on a regular basis.

Consequently one has to add that "fantasy literature depicts things which are contrary to the prevailing ideas of reality, rather than which are incontestably supernatural or impossible" (Grenby 145-6). Accordingly, *Harry Potter* is a fantasy novel, because it includes not only wizardry, but also mythical creatures such as Thestrals or Unicorns. Nevertheless it is important to take into consideration that although fantasy depicts something 'unreal', fantasy must not be regarded as excluding reality, because fantasy and realism are by no means "exclusive categories" (Grenby 146) but can embody realistic anxieties. This is also what makes *Harry Potter* so interesting and valuable for analysis, because it connects aspects of history and reality with fantasy, giving it to the reader to find parallels. Moreover, it invites to cross-reading and symbolic-reading, two more strategies chosen for the following text-oriented analysis (see chapters 3; 4).

As exemplified above, the study of fantasy novels is more complex than it might seem at first sight. Furthermore, within the fantasy genre one distinguishes between 'High Fantasy', which implies the creation of a separate world in which the action takes place, and 'Low Fantasy', where the story is "set in the world we know" (Grenby 144). Here again difficulties arise, trying to assign *Harry Potter* to only one of these categories because the main plot is primarily taking place at Hogwarts, a boarding school only for wizards far away from the non-magic civilization, which can be seen as a separate world, where the daily life includes ghosts and magic. Still in the process of the series, the action is more and more set in the world we know and even taking influence on the 'normal' non-wizarding world. The Ministry of Magic and the Diagon Alley, a shopping avenue for wizards and witches, for example are settled in the middle of London just hidden from the eyes of Muggles, people who cannot perform magic. Due to these aspects, I would assign *Harry Potter* to both, 'High' and 'Low' fantasy and even overlapping with the famous school story. Additionally one can assign the *Harry Potter* series to the 'Ptolemaic fantasy', for which it is typical that the "child characters become more powerful and important, although in their real worlds, they have been weak" (Grenby 160). Also Harry Potter himself is a subordinate in his so-called "home world[s]" (Grenby 160), where he is being treated like a worthless creature, not even deserving an own room with a real bed, but having to sleep in a cupboard under the stairs. But as soon as he enters the fantasy world, he is famous and it will turn out that "no less than the fate of the world rests on [his] their shoulders" (Grenby 160).

In conclusion, Joanne K. Rowling's *Harry Potter* series are not only written for children, but also an educated reader will "appreciate it on different level" (Sullivan 311). Whereas children can be called 'naive readers', not being able to transfer knowledge of the daily life to the book, the adult reader is able to detect intertextual references and draw connections between 'real life' and the life presented in the novels. As emphasized before, children's fantasy books offer an insight to culture and sociology, and are therefore important for cultural studies. My approach to the series is therefore text-oriented as well as reader-based, finding parallels between historical events and events taking place in the fictionalized world.

3. Race

Ever since Bernier's attempt to construct the first "racial classification of mankind" in an article published in the *Journal de Savants* in 1684 (Collier's 587), people have tried to divide human beings into different groupings according to what they believed makes them different from one another. When talking about race[1] and later about racism, it is important to distinguish between the different definitions of race. In general, one has to note that the definitions of race have changed over the past decades and that they focused on different aspects such as physical characteristics, psychological criteria, genetics, or blood types. I have chosen the following definitions of race not only because they are the only ones that are at least to an extend scientifically verifiable, but also because they reflect the wide gap between actual definitions and highly objective ones that were and still are misused to discriminate others.

In biological terms, race is a "biological grouping within the human species, distinguished or classified according to genetically transmitted differences" (Encyclopaedia Britannica 876). This means that a person's DNA has to be examined in order to assign him or her to a specific 'race'. Although it might be fairly easy to distinguish a "North European from a West African Negro" (Collier's 588) just from the physical appearance, it is far more difficult, if not impossible to assign a "population such as the Germans, the French, or the English to any of the specific races into which Europeans have been subdivided" (Collier's 589). By simply looking at the outward appearance of a person it is impossible to draw exact conclusions about his or her 'race' because "the pattern of human variation is predominantly one of within-group variation, so that it is impossible delineate clear boundaries between groups" (Cambridge Encyclopedia 885).

---

[1] The word race without inverted commas only serves the purpose of classification and is not intended to be negatively connoted, whereas ,'race' in inverted commas should stress the fact that at this point race would be used in a negative way by the authors of the works I have analyzed

The '"traditional racial" (Cambridge Encyclopedia 885) classification goes hand in hand with the previous definition, but puts less stress on the genetic pool of humans.

In the Cambridge Encyclopedia (885) it is stated that race

> typically emphasize [s] external features such as skin color or hair type, but other genetically-determined traits such as blood groups or enzyme variants tend to cross-cut the classical categories based on superficial features.

In this definition only the outward appearance determines to which race someone belongs. Nevertheless, assigning someone to a certain race just by the physical appearance and without taking into consideration his genetic pool is no longer reliable, because people have mixed their biological strains as colonization and emigration progressed (Collier's 588). Nevertheless, this type of separation is still predominant in some parts of the world, where people have to give detailed information about whether they are African- American, Caucasian etc. and it is perceived as similar to stating whether you are male or female. Furthermore, "a race in its strict zoological sense is a subdivision of a species, and its criteria are primarily, if not exclusively, anatomical features" (Encyclopaedia Britannica 587). This definition of race is very important because it is "the only one that can be recognized scientifically" (Encyclopaedia Britannica 587).

As one can see, the main definitions of race typically include a division by genetic differences, which have an effect on the outward appearance of the person, but do not define the character of a person or a race in general. Additionally one can observe in the definitions that race is something that a person is born with because his genes and his representations assign him to a certain race. Though it has to be noted that in all Encyclopedias the aspect of race was often closely connected to words like "racism", "controversy" and "uncertain" (Collier's 588), demonstrating that the field of racial research is not as precise and scientific as it might seem. When looking at aspects of race and racism in the *Third Reich* and in *Harry Potter*, it is important to keep these scientific

9

and verifiable approaches to what race actually is in mind, because it will be shown that Adolf Hitler and also Lord Voldemort have a different opinion on what races are, how one can distinguish them and especially how one should treat them.

3.1 Aspect of Race in the *Third Reich*: Hitler's beliefs

For Adolf Hitler, who ruled in Germany for almost 12 years, and whose ideas on 'race' and 'racial purity' have shaped a whole country, the major racial distinction had to be made between the superior 'Aryans'[2] and the inferior 'Jews', which were claimed to be the exact opposite of 'the Aryan' (Geary 7). He based his division not only on the biological, but also on a very questionable psychological definition of 'race', that was proposed by the French ethnologist Joseph-Arthur, comte de Gobineau. He was the first to "attribute a profound value to race in the interpretation of history and biography" (Collier's 587) and moreover the first one to assign psychological and personality attributes to various races which were also "regarded as determinative in the rise and fall of nations and empires" (Collier's 588).

As Hitler ascribed specific personality attributes to Jews as well as Aryans, he made use of this psychological definition of race. He used this pseudo-scientific definition in order to create an enemy who would be hated by the Germans on the one hand, and to form a community that is united in his national identity as 'the superior Aryans' on the other hand. To him this definition served as a proof for his anti-Semitic believes, as well as instrument for his later propaganda. Concerning the 'evil characteristics' of Jews, he was of the opinion that "the Jew was incapable of sacrificing himself for greater, communal good; he was materialistic and untouched by

---

[2] In the following chapters I will use the terms 'Aryan(s)' and 'Jew(s)' 'with inverted commas when specifically emphasizing that at this point they would be or were used in an overgeneralized and negative or positive way by National Socialists
These terms without inverted commas are nevertheless not meant offensively but serve as root term for people of Jewish faith and Aryan background

idealism" (Geary 7). Additionally he wrote in *Mein Kampf* that Jews possessed "eine oft himmelschreiende Borniertheit, die nur durch die manchmal geradezu erstaunliche Einbildung übertroffen wird" (Hitler 352). Hitler's proclamation that 'the Jew' was an embodiment of pure evil who had to be destroyed before he could destroy the 'Aryan race' gets underlined by him declaring that the personification of the devil as image of all evil takes on the shape of 'the Jew' (Hitler 355). By stating that Jewishness is not a matter of religion, but rather inherited and therefore biologically determined, Hitler uses 'scientific evidence' to justify and promote his anti-Semitism (Geary 7).

One can observe that in the *Third Reich* it was created a certain negative image of the 'typical Jew' by assigning to him characteristics that were not valued in German society at that time. 'The Jew' became a scapegoat for everything bad that had happened to Germany in the past, such as the First World War (Geary 7). Furthermore, Jews were "likened to rats, vermin, disease, the plague, germs, bacilli" (Geary 7), all things that one has to eliminate because they bring sickness and decay. A quote which underlines this, as well as it serves as the basis for the systematic killings of many thousand Jews can be found in Dick Geary's *Hitler and Nazism*, where it is indicated that "Jews did not have to be treated as human beings. If Jews were 'vermin', then they were to be treated as such: that is, eradicated" (Geary 8).

On the other hand, Hitler used the psychological definition of race in a rather positive way, in terms that he assigned personal characteristics to Aryans that were perceived as positive by society and which should unite the Germans. Hitler based the superiority of the Aryan race on the fact that they embodied valuable characteristics for society, such as "the capacity for work, the fulfillment of public duty, self-sacrifice and idealism" (Geary 7). These positive qualities of 'the Aryans' were also "not created by society, but were genetically determined" (Geary 7), such as Jews were genetically determined to be brutal and without any moral concerns (Hitler

11

354). Moreover, he underlined the superiority of 'the Aryan race' by pointing out how much the Germans had endured and survived historically. Taking into consideration the widely spread idea of social Darwinism with its theory about the 'Survival of the Fittest', the Germans were predestined to rule over others because they have been able to win out over all threats (Encyclopaedia Britannica).

However, Hitler did not only assign specific characteristics to Jews and Aryans, based on inherited and 'scientifically proven' psychological and personality attributes typical for 'their race'. He additionally linked these values to the rise and fall of nations and empires, as it was also defined in *Gobineau's* definition of race (Collier's 588). In *Mein Kampf*, Hitler stated that:

> The peoples of the world could be divided into three racial groups: the creators of culture, the bearers of culture (people who can imitate the creations of the superior race), and inferior peoples who are the 'destroyers of culture' (Geary 6-7).

As a matter of course 'the Aryans' were declared to be the creators of culture because they managed to build small and well-organized groups, full of ambition to sacrifice themselves for the communal good and who "conquered larger numbers of inferior people and brought to them the values of culture" (Geary 7). 'Jews' on the other hand were viewed as the destroyers of cultures and therefore inferior to 'the Aryan'.

After having pointed out by which evolutionary theories and racial definitions Hitler was inspired and which were used to justify his later procedures, it is important to recall the definitions of race made in the previous chapter. As explained in the introduction to the topic of race and its definitions, the only definition that is scientifically verifiable, is based on genetic differences. Neither differentiation by psychological and personality attributes, nor by interpretation of history and biography can be proven scientifically. Moreover, these practices are highly dubious and there is "no evidence for biologically-determined differences between populations in such ability or character traits" (Cambridge Enzyclopedia 885).

12

Consequently the genes are not responsible for personality and character of people, but the environment, which influences and shapes them. Furthermore, "personality is an elusive thing, difficult to measure with scientific objectivity and reliability, and at that period there was not even a scientific method available for the procedure" (Collier's 588). Hitler basically based his whole ideology on "more or less superficial reading of history and the uncritical use of culture" (Collier's 588).

3.2 The *Pure- Blood Agenda– Racial Hygiene* as a Consequence of Racial Hatred in the *Third Reich*

Even though Hitler's beliefs could not be proven scientifically, they still influenced and shaped a whole society. What started out basically as an idea of 'superiority' and 'inferiority' soon developed into racial hatred and the "furchtbarste Verbrechen der Weltgeschichte" (Hofer 80) as the systematic mass killings of Jews and others who were of no 'biological value' for the community were called (Geary 60).

As mentioned before, Jews became scapegoats for the poor economic situation of Germany after the war and furthermore everything else that did not go its right way in society was blamed onto them (Aleff 79). Racist and anti-Semitist beliefs, today also known as 'rechtes Gedankengut', manifested themselves within society and in order to 'benefit' society, Hitler promoted the deportation and the killings of Jews. As some scientists claim, "Die Vernichtung der Juden Europas war das zentrale Ziel seiner Politik" (Hildebrand 82). But for Hitler it was not enough to only 'clean' the country from Jews, he furthermore wanted to 'wipe out' all traces of Jewish blood because he believed that „[a]lle großen Kulturen der Vergangenheit gingen nur zu Grunde, weil die ursprünglich schöpferische Rasse an Blutvergiftung abstarb" (Hitler 316). Here again comte de Gobineau had built the theoretical 'proof' and 'basis' for these

views in his famous *Essai sur l'inégalité des races humaines,* 4 vol, by
stating that:

> the fate of civilizations is determined by racial composition, that
> white and in particular Aryan societies flourish as long as they
> remain free of black and yellow strains, and that the more a
> civilization's racial character is diluted through miscegenation, the
> more likely it is to lose its vitality and creativity and sink into
> corruption and immorality (Encyclopaedia Britannica).

An "Orden des guten Blutes" (Himmler 31) should be created and the
blood of the Jewish spilled "zum Heile der germanischen Rasse" (Hofer
268). As a result of these understandings, the so-called 'pure-blood
agenda', which promoted marriage between Aryans and condemned
interracial mixing with Aryans and Jews, came into being. Hitler wanted to
prevent intermingling between Aryans and Jews and by establishing the
Law for the Defense of German Blood, he "prohibited marriage and sexual
relations between Jews and non-Jews" (Geary 74). The *Blutsreinheit*
became more important because it was assumed that "die verlorene
Blutsreinheit allein zerstört das innere Glück für immer, senkt den
Menschen für ewig nieder, und die Folgen sind niemals mehr aus Körper
und Geist zu beseitigen" (Hitler 359). Children that resulted from
relationships between an Aryan and a Jew, called 'Mischlinge', were also
declared as dangerous. Extremists even argued that "partial Jews were
more dangerous than full Jews because their mix of German and Jewish
blood would enable them to lead the state's enemies with the skill of
Aryans" (Noakes, Pridham). By crossing Aryan and Jewish bloodlines and
"sin[ning] against the blood" (Geary 7), Hitler believed Germany sealed its
doom. The mixing of the master race with its inferiors in his eyes, "led to
racial deterioration and inevitable decay" (Geary 7).

Consequently Hitler saw "die "Ausrottung des jüdischen Volkes"
(Hildebrand 83) and the cleaning of the impure as his mission in order to
prevent Germany's downfall. Racial hygiene, cleaning the race by

exterminating poisoning blood, was promoted and caused the death of millions of innocent people.

3.3 Race in *Harry Potter*: Wizards and Muggles

Also in Joanne K. Rowling's *Harry Potter* series, the aspect of belonging to a certain 'race' plays a major role and is a recurring theme in each of her novels. The major distinction made here is the distinction between Muggles, people who are not able to perform magic, and wizards. Although it is important to point out that in the series, racial differentiation and prejudices work in both directions, the following outline will focus on the categorizations made by wizards, or to be more precise, by wizards believing that their ability to perform magic makes them superior to others.

Lord Voldemort, the main villain in Joanne K. Rowling's *Harry Potter* series, is one of those wizards who believe that his ability to do magic makes him superior to Muggles. Although nobody knows how magical abilities are being passed on, he feels to be benefitted with this ability for a reason, namely to "establish a wizard rule over Muggles" (Rowling Hallows, 292). Similarly to Hitler, who believed that 'the Aryan race' was destined to rule over 'the Jews' due to their ability to create culture, Voldemort believed that, as the slogan, "Magic is Might" (Rowling Hallows 294) suggests, wizards were to rule over Muggles because of their magical skills. In his point of view, wizards were born with the "right to rule" (Rowling Hallows 294) and the fact that all actions, no matter how cruel or inhuman, were done for "the Greater Good" (Rowling Hallows 294), served as justification.

Also Voldemort assumed that the current situation of wizards, namely their separation from the Muggle-world, was the fault of the Muggles who had forced them into hiding (Rowling Hallows 159). Muggles became scapegoats for wizards just like Jews became scapegoats for Aryans. Furthermore, in the eyes of Lord Voldemort and his followers,

Muggles were "like animals, stupid and dirty" (Rowling Hallows 462) which underlines their inferiority and unworthiness of living. "Die gedankliche Nähe zum Faschismus" (Nitzschmann 56) and to the racist beliefs of the *Third Reich* already become visible within this racial distinction. But before analyzing and comparing the effects of the differentiations made within the novels in chapter 3.5 in more detail, the following chapter will briefly introduce an even more precise specification within the wizarding race that is undertaken by Lord Voldemort and his supporters.

3.4 Differentiation between Pure- Blood, Half- Blood and Muggle- Born

It was already hinted at the fact, that the aspect of race is far more complex than it might seem at first sight, when dividing mankind into either Muggles or wizards. Nonetheless, over the course of the novels, the reader comes to know that also within the race of wizards, some people like Lord Voldemort or Lucius Malfoy make further distinctions. By considering the "blood status" (Rowling Hallows 207), one can namely make subcategories within the wizarding race and divide wizards into Pure-blood wizards, Half-blood wizards and Muggle-born wizards.

As the name already reveals, Pure-bloods such as Draco Malfoy come from a family that is claimed to be free from Muggle-blood. Families, such as the Blacks or the Malfoys, who were very proud of their noble heritage, tried to only marry other Pure-bloods to preserve their royalty (Rowling Order 104). If members did not do as they were told, they were simply erased from the family tree and so their blood stayed 'clean' from bad and poisoning blood (Rowling Order 105). As a consequence, the race of Pure-bloods was often times seen as the wizarding elite. Half- bloods, such as Harry Potter on the other hand come from families with Muggles as well as wizards as their closest relatives. Within the hierarchy of blood-purity, the Half-bloods were one level below the Pure-bloods, but still despised by them and often times called "half-breeds" (Rowling Order 96). At the bottom of the hierarchy were the Muggle-borns, often referred to as "Mudbloods" (Rowling Order 100), such as Hermione Granger, who are able to perform magic even though their parents were both Muggles. Despite the fact that Muggle-borns are at the bottom of the wizard hierarchy, they are nevertheless lumped together as inferiors with Half-bloods.

Summing up, this differentiation basically assigns wizards to categories through ancestor research, implementing that based on even these, people are more or less worthy to belong to the wizarding society, no matter how talented they really are. The similarities between the differentiations made in the Nuremberg laws from 1935, where Jews were divided into "Volljuden" and "Halbjuden" are impossible to ignore at that point (Nürnberger Gesetze), and the consequences these differentiations had for wizards will be examined in the following chapter.

3.5 *Racial Hygiene* as Result of Racism in *Harry Potter*

However, putting wizards into categories and therefore establishing a hierarchy within the race of wizards did not remain without consequences. The following chapter will hence reveal the effects of these differentiations and compare them to the consequences the labeling of Jews had during the *Third Reich*. Before going into more detail, it is central to make clear that I will use the term Mudblood, although it has a negative connotation and often times used to insult non-pure blood wizards, as root category for Muggle-borns to make the differences more visible. Additionally it is important to point out that for Lord Voldemort and his like- minded people, Muggles and Muggle-borns were all "filthy" (Rowling Order 104) and subordinate creatures that had to be suppressed and erased.

As shown in the previous chapter, pure-blood wizards often times thought themselves as superior to Muggles and Mudbloods due to their ability to do magic, but especially because of their family background. Led by Lord Voldemort, whose reign can be compared to Hitler's reign in Germany because both "Schreckensregime" (Nitzschmann 25) were filled with the dissemination of terror and fear, likewise Muggles and Mudbloods were not only bullied and insulted, but also tortured and killed for "THE GREATER GOOD" (Rowling Order 192). Similarly to Hitler, the Dark Lord namely believed that the mixing of the superior Pure-bloods with the dirty and unworthy Mudbloods, "led to racial deterioration and inevitable decay" (Geary 7). As a consequence one had to "cut away those parts that threaten the health of the rest" (Rowling Hallows 17). The fact that also Lord Voldemort and his followers planned the systematic killings of 'unworthy' wizards and Muggles becomes very clear in this statement.

By assigning negative characteristics to Muggle-borns and placing them on the same level as animals, Lord Voldemort had also created an enemy that was claimed to pose great dangers to the "peaceful Pure-blood society" (Rowling Hallows 205) and therefore had to be eliminated. Additionally to making Muggles and Mudbloods appear in a bad light due to their general 'unworthiness', he deprived them of their identity by calling them animals or beasts (Rowling Hallows 16). Furthermore this gets underlined by the fact that wizards from Muggle origin were, equally to people from Jewish origin in the *Third Reich*, no longer called by their names but were only being referred to as "the Jew" (Aleff 79) and "the Mudblood" (Rowling Order 101). Their identity was now overshadowed by negative characteristics, making it easier for people to unite against and to hate them for 'what' they obviously were: "unheimlich und eigentlich gar nicht mehr [ein] vollwertiger Mensch" (Aleff 79).

Likewise Hitler and his followers, Lord Voldemort and his Death Eaters believed that the wizarding race should be cleaned from "filthy half-breeds" because the pureblood "is the only kind of wizard worth being" (Rowling Order 96; 742). In their eyes, the wizarding race had to be cleaned from "canker that infects us until only those of the true blood remain" (Rowling Hallows 17). This racist and fascist thinking manifested itself in parts of the wizarding world and developed into a "pure-blood mania", trying to "get rid of Muggle-borns and having Pure-bloods in charge (Rowling Order 104). Like the Jews, Mudbloods were regarded as fair game, and whoever killed them, benefitted society. The "purification of the wizarding race" (Rowling Order 104), which has become the main goal during the reign of Lord Voldemort, resulted from these views and categorizations and caused the death of many Muggles and Muggle-borns.

In conclusion one can record that also in the fictional wizarding world of the *Harry Potter* series, the attempt to categorize people according to their abilities and therefore establishing a clear hierarchy leads to prejudices, hatred and feelings of superiority. As in the *Third Reich*, these racist beliefs found their expression in racial hygiene and the systematic elimination of people that were hated only because their blood was considered to be 'not clean' and poisonous for the health of society.

4. Parallels between the *Third Reich* and the World presented in J.K. Rowling's *Harry Potter and the Order of the Phoenix*

Already in the first part of my thesis, the aspect of race and how supposedly 'subordinates' were treated within the *Harry Potter* series have shown remarkable parallels towards the practices in the *Third Reich*. Dick Geary underlines these findings and sums them up by stating that:

> Nazi society underwent significant change as a result of racial policy is indisputable. The life chances of its citizens depended more upon their race and 'racial purity' than on any other single fact (Geary 62).

Nevertheless, society underwent not only changes in terms of race. Furthermore the adaptations of new laws and regulations for the German population in general have changed immensely during the reign of Adolf Hitler. Similarly one can detect such constitutional changes in Joanne K. Rowling's *Harry Potter and the Order of the Phoenix*. The following chapters will therefore focus on these parallels and point out the effects such political and constitutional changes had on society.

4.1 Infiltration of the School System

As Hogwarts in *Harry Potter* and schools in general play a major role in the development of children because they form the next generation, schools have always been an important tool to shape society. Hitler and the government in *the Order of the Phoenix* have made use of this valuable tool and sent like- minded followers into the schools to teach the young generation their values and to shape them according to their needs.

In *Harry Potter and the Order of the Phoenix* for example, the Ministry of Magic seeks educational reform by appointing Dolores Umbridge, a witch that is equally popular with the Minister of Magic, Cornelius Fudge, and Lord Voldemort, the "First ever High Inquisitor" (Rowling Order 274). Officially Cornelius Fudge gave her permission and order to "inspect her fellow educators" and to provide the Minister with "on-the-ground feedback of what's really happening at school" due to the "falling standards in at Hogwarts" (Rowling Order 275). By making her first High Inquisitor, the Ministry unofficially gave "itself an unprecedented level of control at Hogwarts School of Witchcraft and Wizardry" (Rowling Order 274). As it will be analyzed and pointed out in the course of this chapter, Dolores Umbridge therefore served the Ministry of Magic in many ways.

First and foremost she functioned as a spy, reporting everything she heard or saw to the Ministry. She even monitored "all channels in and out of Hogwarts" (Rowling Order 556), scanning letters from students and looking for any kind of resistance against the Ministry. When she found out that someone was criticizing her or starting an attempt to revolt against the new ways of teaching, she threatened them with detention (Rowling Order 511). Here one can detect the first great conformity with actions taken in the *Third Reich*, where the *Verordnung des Reichspräsidenten zum Schutze von Volk und Staat* (28.02 1933) brought profound changes to the personal freedom as it declared "Eingriffe in das Brief, -Post-, Telegraphen- und Fernsprechgeheimnis" (Reichsgesetzblatt 1933, 83) to be admissible. In the eyes of the government this was a very necessary action in order to repel subversive actions by Communists.

Further Dolores Umbridge was exploited to ensure that only "a Ministry-approved curriculum" (Rowling Order 216) was taught. Ruling with an iron grip, she carried out highly prejudiced investigations on her fellow teachers, "looking for an excuse to get rid of teachers she thinks are too close to Dumbledore" (Rowling Order 388-9), because she and the Minister were afraid that Dumbledore would build an army of students and teachers to overthrow the Ministry. For Adolf Hitler it was similarly important to interfere in the school system and change the curriculum to have the next generation raised "im neuen Geiste" and according to the new "NS-Weltanschauung" (Giesecke, 7) so they would not question his government and revolt against him. Furthermore they should be taught his values of obedience, respect and self-sacrifice for the state from their

21

earliest childhood on, in order to bring up the next generation of good and loyal soldiers that act completely in the sense of the National-Socialists (Hofer 75). In both governments, any kind of disobedience of students or criticism from teachers was directly reported to the head of state and lead to serious consequences. As the example of Professor Trelawney in *Harry Potter* shows, people who do not act and behave like the Ministry wants them to, might not only loose their jobs and professions, but also loose their homes (Rowling Order 524). The threatening of detentions for students, which consisted of corporal punishment, and the threatening of probation for teachers were used as leverage against disobedience. If people wanted to keep their jobs, they had to follow the rules of the Ministry and not question their orders. That way the government put the people in silence and imposed its will on them. In *Die phantastische Welt des Harry Potter*, Karin Nitzschmann concludes that „Die Schule wird zum Spiegel der europäischen Totalitarismus Geschichte. Zu einem Umerziehungslager, indem Dolores Jane Umbridge ein protofaschistisches Regime zu führen beginnt" (118).

Furthermore the new teaching techniques that Umbridge introduces at Hogwarts underline this. As she condemns the practical use of defense spells and refuses to let students do magic, the only thing that can protect them from the Dark Lord, Dolores Umbridge weakens the students by repressing their learning process and keeping them unprepared (Rowling Order 227). In addition to this, her lessons show that students should not make use of their intellect and form their own opinions about what is going on inside and outside of Hogwarts. Instead pupils should simply read about spells and not question or even practice them. Just as in the military, where people receive orders and have to follow them without questioning the sense behind it, Harry and all other pupils were directed to be silent and follow Umbridge's orders (Rowling Order 217). The Ministry again tries to keep the students unprepared for battle, fearing that they might rebel. Umbridge herself proves this perception by stating that she is "here to teach [you] using a Ministry-approved method that does not include inviting students to give their opinions on matters about which they understand little" (Rowling Order 284). So the corridors of Hogwarts "[sind] schon bald [...] von Umbridge's faschistoiden Erlassen zur Unterbindung jeglicher Denk-Freiheit buchstäblich vernagelt" (Kühn 118).

Although Hitler on the other hand wanted his pupils to be trained for combat against hostile countries, he also did not want an intellectual education that encourages students to form their own opinion and rebel against him. In a speech about *Jugenderziehung* he even stated that "mit Wissen verderbe ich mir die Jugend" (Rauschning 237). With this statement he clearly indicated that he wanted to keep the youth as unenlightened as possible so they could not see through his allegedly scientific proofs that "die deutsche Herrenrasse zu herrschen [hat], die minderwertigen Völker zu gehorchen und zu arbeiten [haben] oder gar ausgerottet werden [müssen]" (Zimmermann 73), an argument produced to justify not only the start of the Second World War, but also to justify the deportation and killings of the Jewish population living in Germany. Here again both governments interfere in the school system to form pupils at their needs and to suppress them in their own ability to think independently.

In addition, Dolores Umbridge was sent to Hogwarts in order to correct what teachers before her had done wrong and to "make those necessary changes that the Ministry so ardently desires" (Rowling Order 267). Meaning not only that she should change the curriculum into one that is officially "Ministry approved" (Rowling Order 216), but also that she should put greater emphasis on values such as discipline, obedience and respect which are claimed to have been neglected by previous teachers. Students in her class for example had to always raise their hands before they speak and address her as "Professor Umbridge" (Rowling Order 216) showing her respect. Adolf Hitler had put much emphasis on the same values in his strict education because to him the political strength of a society did not lie within "einer größtmöglichen Geistigkeit der Mitglieder [liegt] als vielmehr im disziplinierten Gehorsam mit dem ihre Mitglieder der geistigen Führung Gefolgschaft leisten" (Hitler 510). If people were not disciplined and obedient, this could cause the downfall of the empire.

Both governments therefore made great scholarly changes, as they reinforced strict rules of discipline and discouraged students to form their own opinion. Every aspect of school life was under their personal control and took place for the sole purpose of serving and securing their government. The violation of basic individual rights such as the freedom of speech, were eventually accepted because they exclusively served "for the Greater Good" (Rowling Hallows 194). It is furthermore important to bear in mind that within the *Third Reich* these changes did not only take place in the schools but influenced daily life of people in Germany. School was but one aspect of many that the Nazis have brought under their control.

4.2 Adaptation of new Laws– Educational Decrees

In order to benefit and secure this government and for the welfare of the state in general, the heads of state did not only interfere in the school system, furthermore new laws had to be adapted to restrict the public and to defeat the enemies. During the reign of Adolf Hitler, the whole political system was restructured and many new laws, from which the Nuremberg Laws were probably the most famous as they marked "a major step in clarifying racial policy and removing Jewish influences from Aryan society" (Jewishlibrary) were enacted. Since Hogwarts is the main setting of Joanne K. Rowling's novels, such restrictive laws were firstly adapted there before they were extended to the wizarding world in general. Within Hogwarts they were known as "Educational Decrees" (Rowling Order 275), arranged from the Minister of Magic and enforced by Dolores Umbridge. Again these Educational Decrees share a lot of common features with the laws enacted in the Germany because High Inquisitor Dolores Umbridge "setzt schrittweise ein brutales und totalitäres Regime durch" (Nitzschmann 118). It is of great importance to make clear that these actions were taken by the Ministry of Magic out of the fear of being overthrown by Albus Dumbledore and his supporters and not because Cornelius Fudge wanted a wizarding society free from Muggleblood. The following chapters will therefore present and oppose the Educational Decrees in *Harry Potter and the Order of the Phoenix* with the laws established by Adolf Hitler and his members of parliament in the *Third Reich*.

4.2.1 Educational Decree Number Twenty-four

A few days after the first meeting of *Dumbledore's Army*, a group of students that gathered to "learn Defense Against the Dark Arts" (Rowling Order 312) from Harry, Educational Decree Number Twenty- four was released. The order of the High Inquisitor of Hogwarts stated that:

> All student organizations, societies, teams, groups and clubs are henceforth disbanded. An organization, society team, group or club is hereby defined as a regular meeting of three or more students. Permission to re-form may be sought from the High Inquisitor (Professor Umbridge). No student organization, society, team, group or club may exist without the knowledge and approval of the High Inquisitor. Any student found to have formed, or to belong to, an organization, society, team, group or club that has not been approved by the High Inquisitor will be expelled (Rowling Order 13).

By releasing this Decree, the government made sure that students were not gathering to plan a plot against the Ministry or to practice in dueling. Moreover, all attempts to form resistance groups should be destroyed at birth. The fact that pupils could be expelled if they acted against this order was used as leverage, putting those who really planned a resistance movement under very high pressure. Of course organizations that were lead by people in favor of the government because their members were opponents of Albus Dumbledore, such as the Slytherin Quidditch Team were not only allowed but also encouraged (Rowling Order 354). As the example of Professor Snape, who "was turning a deaf ear to the many reports of Slytherin attempts to hex Gryffindor players in the corridors" (Rowling Order 354) shows, these favored groups were also exploited to demoralize and harass their opponents. The fact that Dolores Umbridge also set up her own "Inquisitorial Squad" (Rowling Order 551), students whom she picked out herself to observe other students and to punish them for any kind of misbehavior underlines her control mania for the 'greater good'. As the example of Draco Malfoy, who takes ten points off from Gryffindor, just because Hermione is a 'Mudblood' shows, within these groups positions are often misused. He, as well as other Slytherins took every chance they could get to bully other students and to make their lives hard. Especially 'muggle-borns' had to suffer their attacks and their discriminations, such as Jews were bullied and harassed by members of the *Hitlerjugend*. Despite the fact that pupils were now observing and telling on their classmates, the Ministry also kept them busy, hindering them from questioning the actions taken by the government.

In the *Third Reich*, Adolf Hitler used a similar method to minimize the risk of a resistance movement and to increase his power. On July 14th 1933 the *Gesetz gegen die Neubildung von Parteien* entered into force, which on the one hand ensured the one-party state as it declared other political parties than the NSDAP illegal and on the other hand dissolved independent pressure groups (Geary 40). Similarly to Dolores Umbridge who was claimed to have a "furious desire to bring every aspect of life at Hogwarts under her personal control" (Rowling Order 487), Adolf Hitler also wanted full control over state and society. Robert Ley, a leading politician of the NSDAP stresses this as he says:

> Dieses Organisationsmonopol geht darauf aus, den Mann im Volke völlig unselbständig zu machen, jede wie immer geartete Initiative zu den primitivsten freiwilligen Zusammenschlüssen in ihm zu ertöten, ihn von allen Gleichgesinnten oder auch nur Gleichgestimmten fernzuhalten, ihn zu isolieren und zugleich an die staatliche Organisation zu binden (Michalka 95).

People that thought like the government should consequently come together and be joined in governmental organizations to strengthen the state, but differently thinking people should be isolated and not be given a chance to come together to build an opposition. Here as well we can find a "campaign of violence against its political opponents", where members of oppositional parties were "beaten up" (Geary 39). Ten thousands of Communists and Social Democrats, which have built the largest oppositional parties at that time and who were perceived as a great threat towards the NSDAP "were detained and some were tortured or murdered" (Geary 39). The threat of the use of violence and detentions was used as an additional amplifier to hinder pressure groups from assembling and rebelling.

In conclusion one can say about *Educational Decree Number Twenty-four* and the *Gesetz gegen die Neubildung von Parteien* that they primarily had a control function as they did not make it possible for people to join together and stand up for themselves (Geary 42). "The destruction of independent organizations in the *Third Reich*" and also in *The Order of the Phoenix* "simply obliterated the necessary framework for action" (Geary 42) and was consequently an insurance to keep the risk of being overthrown by resistance groups as low as possible.

4.2.2 Educational Decree Number Twenty-five

Educational Decree Number Twenty- five, which states that: "The High Inquisitor has to have the power to strip pupils privileges, or she would have less authority than common teachers!" (Rowling Order 368) is another law to underline how much power the Ministry has gained over the school, its pupils and its 'actual' teachers. Again we find here that the Ministry tries to gain control not only over all aspects of school life. To emphasize the seizing power even more, *Educational Decree Number Twenty-five* also says that:

The High Inquisitor will henceforth have supreme authority over all punishments, sanctions and removal of privileges pertaining to the students of Hogwarts, and the power to alter such punishments, sanctions and removals of privileges as may have been ordered by other staff members (Rowling Order 368-9).

Umbridge therefore has the right to contradict all teachers in their decision-making and to punish students only according to her own system of values. Concerning the punishments one can observe here that Umbridge misused her authority greatly as she made use of a special "thin black quill with an unusually sharp point" that cuts the texts pupils had to write during detention into their skins "as though traced there by a scalpel" (Rowling Order 240) even though corporal punishment was not allowed at Hogwarts. The brutality of this kind of punishment gets emphasized by the fact that the lines themselves were not written with ink, but with the blood of the pupils, cutting the message deeper and deeper into their skin (Rowling Order 241). Torturing pupils so they did not speak up and raise their voice against the Ministry became a popular method for Umbridge to oppress pupils and to gain more control over them.

Furthermore we find a strong misuse of authority as she makes the very prejudiced and one-sided decision to ban Harry Potter and Ron Weasley from Quidditch after they had started a fight with Draco Malfoy, who had insulted members of their families (Rowling Order 369). Given the fact that Draco Malfoy, whose father is a known Death Eater and who has never made a secret out of the fact that he detests Muggle-borns, did not get punished, but rather rewarded, as his opponents were disciplined underlines this misuse. In addition to that Ron's twin brothers Fred and George were also banned from Quidditch without even having attacked Malfoy, but mainly because Umbridge predicted that they "would have attacked young Mr. Malfoy as well" (Rowling Order 369) if they had not been restrained by their teammates. People could consequently be punished even before they had actually done anything wrong. This anticipatory nature of sanctions and its arbitrariness made life at Hogwarts

28

very unpredictable. To carry it to an extreme, one could make the assertion that Umbridge established a totalitarian state at Hogwarts, where she had brought every aspect of the student's lives under her control.

The fact that *Educational Decree Number Twenty-five* was later extended and gave clear permission to whip students without stating under which circumstances the whippings were allowed underlines once more the arbitrariness of such actions (Rowling Order 593) and fueled the fear of corporal punishments within the school. Because students now had to watch every step they took even more closely, this Educational Decree was a helpful device to silence and suppress students. This tyranny at Hogwarts can as well be compared to the "institutionalized terror" in the *Third Reich*, where the "slightest show of dissent was [also] likely to be met with a beating, with arrest and imprisonment, or with incarceration in a concentration camp (Geary 42). Furthermore also Hitler and his followers tried to get every aspect of personal and public life under their control, using "comprehensive and systematic brutality" against its opponents and establishing a state that "rested exclusively on terror and intimidation" (Geary 43). The *Verordnung des Reichspräsidenten zum Schutz von Volk und Staat* justified these actions, as they were declared necessary for the "Abwehr kommunistischer staatsgefährdender Gewaltakte" (Reichsgesetzblatt 1933 Nr.17, 83). Again, violence and intimidation are justified with only serving the 'greater good' of the state and its inhabitants. By intimidating and threatening the German population with physical abuse, imprisonment and even death the Nazis kept them under control and extended their influence in all spheres of public life.

Another similarity between the procedures in Joanne K. Rowling's novel and actions taken by the National Socialists in the *Third Reich* lies within their 'anticipatory nature'. As the example of the Weasley twins has shown, they could be punished before they had even done anything wrong. Similar to that, "people [in the Third Reich] could [also] be arrested before they had done anything" (Geary 43) which made oppression even more successful. Although these actions were claimed to take place "based on a systematic and ubiquitous surveillance of the population" (Geary 43), they were nevertheless arbitrary and unpredictable for the population who often had to fear military interventions.

To conclude, this chapter has presented that in *Harry Potter and the Order of the Phoenix* and in the *Third Reich*, the government has established a regime of intimidation and violence to gain control over society and thus to secure their own power. Additionally, laws that justified cruelty towards people were modified or brought into being which shaped society immensely. Certainly both rulerships also had their followers and supporters without whom the system would not have worked. From the findings presented one can nevertheless assume that without these major constitutional changes, the power to adjust the laws according to their demands and without a campaign of violence against their opponents, both governments would have not been so successful. Consequently one can summarize brutality, oppression and intimidation with the threat of violence as the key components of those totalitarian governments and unpredictable states.

4.2.3 Educational Decree Number Twenty-seven

By legislating the *Educational Decree Number Twenty-seven*, the Minister of Magic and Dolores Umbridge took another essential step towards gaining full control over the pupils at Hogwarts and to suffocate any kind of resistance from the beginning as they restricted the freedom of the press.

Because controlling the newspapers and using it to spread only the news that are in the government's favor was and still is used successfully to make people believe what they should believe and to hinder free formation and expression of opinion, it was also an integral part of Cornelius Fudge's and Adolf Hitler's rule. In Joanne K. Rowling's novel, the reader first gets to know that the *Daily Prophet*, the main newspaper for witches and wizards, operates under the authority of the Ministry and was misused to launch smear campaigns about people that could threaten the system (Rowling Order 71). But as a small and independent newspaper called *The Quibbler* published an article stating that the Dark Lord has returned and already killed one student, consequently contradicting everything the *Daily Prophet* has tried to convince the people of, the Ministry saw it as its responsibility to take action and declare the possession of *The Quibbler* illegal (Rowling Order 512). By legislating *Educational Decree Number Twenty-seven*, which stated that:" Any student found in the possession of the magazine *The Quibbler* will be expelled" (Rowling Order 512), the Ministry of Magic even took its influence one step further than 'simply' manipulating the media as it made the possession of an 'oppositional newspaper' punishable. As a result not only the freedom of the press in general was limited but also the public was severely restricted. This Decree was another important law to suppress all opposition and also a famous method used in the *Third Reich*, where

> Presse und Rundfunk insbesondere [einer strengen Staatskontrolle unterstellt wurden], und ein ‚Schriftleitergesetz' [die Handhabe bieten sollte], missliebige Persönlichkeiten aus der publizistischen Arbeit herauszuhalten (Reichsgesetzblatt Nr. 111, 713).

The media in the *Third Reich* were consequently also an instrument of might that was taken over and used to shape and influence society in two ways: on the one hand to "mobilize the minds of the people behind the Führer through active propaganda" (Geary 41) and on the other hand to restrict the peoples knowledge about things that were really happening at that time. As a result, these methods equate to brainwash and therefore make the media another powerful instrument which both governments have taken possession of to control the masses.

4.3 Friend or Enemy?

As pointed out in the previous chapters, the governments in *Harry Potter* and in the *Third Reich* have achieved to interfere in administration, school, media and the course of justice in order to establish a state in which every aspect of public and social life of its people was under their control. But to secure this control and power over the people they did not only enable laws, furthermore they managed to infiltrate families and to create a society that was filled with mistrust. Through constant monitoring, the misuse of positions, the threat of inflicting harm on people and the specific use of brainwash, both rulers have therefore built an unpredictable nation. In *Harry Potter and the Order of the Phoenix* this unpredictability and lack of trust runs like a continuous thread through the novel.

Firstly many students at Hogwarts mistrusted Harry because the *Daily Prophet* has published several articles in which he and Dumbledore were being ridiculed and accused to be liars. The fact that Seamus Finnigan, who has always been a friend to Harry, Ron and Hermione turns away from them after having read all the negative articles about Harry in the *Daily Prophet* and called Harry a "liar" and "mad" (Rowling Order 197), shows that influencing the media did not miss its intended effect as even between friends great displeasures were now expressed. Because the news were contradicting Harry's assertions of the return of the Dark Lord so convincingly, also some of his actual friends have turned their backs on him. Furthermore Harry and his friends experienced another setback, when Marietta, a member of *Dumbledore's Army* told on them and their secret gatherings, causing the suspension of Hogwarts's headmaster Albus Dumbledore. As one can observe here, nobody knew anymore who was friend and who was enemy, whom they could trust, and whom they could not trust. The circumstances in school and outside of school therefore put them into the position of having to question the loyalty of all their friends and sometimes even their family.

32

The highly manipulative character of the government becomes clearer when considering that even family bonds, such as the Weasley's were torn apart because the parents have looked behind the curtain and did no longer support the Ministry and instead contributed to a resistance group, whereas their son Percy was a blind follower and supporter of the wizarding government. Percy, who had always been very ambitious and very proud that he worked for the Ministry, did not want to see what was really happening and that his "boss was being controlled by Voldemort" (Rowling Order 68). His loyalty lay no longer with his family, but with the Ministry and in order to keep his 'good job' he turned his back on them and betrayed them (Rowling Order 69). Similarly to many children and young adults in Germany, who saw the loyalty towards the state and the National Socialist beliefs as their obligation, Percy left his parents behind for the 'greater good'.

He even makes efforts to tear his family even more apart by advising Ron in a personal letter to "not allow family ties to blind [him] to the misguided nature of [their] parents' beliefs and actions" (Rowling Order 268). Instead of believing and trusting his parents, who Percy claims to be "mixed up with the dangerous crowd around Dumbledore" and "petty criminals" (Rowling Order 267) in general, Ron should rather join with Dolores Umbridge and the Inquisitional Squad. Percy's devotion to the government and Cornelius Fudge, who "could not be more gracious" (Rowling Order 267) to him becomes very clear at that point and underlines the fact that he was able to leave his family behind for the belief in a government. Again, also in the *Third Reich* it was often observed that due to effective propaganda and infiltration of all spheres of personal life by National Socialists "family ties were disrupted and generation set against generation" (Geary 44) because children had more faith in the government than in their relatives. Because children were raised "körperlich, geistig und sittlich im Geiste des Nationalsozialismus, zum Dienst am Volk und zur Volksgemeinschaft" (Reichsgesetzblatt 1936, 993) especially in the Hitler

Youth, their actions against their parents could be justified by serving the country with their betrayal. The fact that

> children indoctrinated in the Hitler Youth or the League of German Maidens could and did report the views of their parents to Nazi officials, who became an alternative source of authority to the parent, priest or schoolteacher (Geary 44)

emphasizes and reflects the infiltration of the government into the private life of families in the *Third Reich* on the one hand and on the other hand reveals that even within families nobody could be sure anymore whom they could trust and truly rely upon.

Besides advising Ron to turn his back on his parents, Percy furthermore tried to convince Ron in his letter, that he should not only spy on his best friend Harry, and report everything to Mrs. Umbridge, he even recommends him to end his friendship with his best friend since "nothing could put [him] in more danger of losing [his] badge more than continued fraternization with that boy" (Rowling Order 266-7). By threatening Ron to loose his honoring prefect badge, which has given him authority and responsibility at school, something that Ron has always wanted, Percy intends to put him into a moral conflict and hopes that Ron's desire to be popular and successful would win over his loyalty towards his friends and his family. To underline his argument and to make spying more tempting for Ron, Percy adds that this would benefit his career prospects as "a student who shows himself willing to help Professor Umbridge now may be well-placed for Head Boyship in a couple of years" (Rowling Order 267). The fact that Ron at this point had to decide between his future career and his friends and beliefs can again be compared to the situation many young men faced in Germany during the reign of Adolf Hitler because there as well a membership in the *Hitlerjugend* and obedience to the state was necessary to start careers in the civil service. Moreover in the *Third Reich* children were also prompted to report misbehavior and views contrary to those of the government to Nazi officials (Geary 44). The situation Ron now faced could additionally be compared to the moral conflict of many

34

Germans that were friends with Jews because before 1914, the "German Jewish community was relatively well integrated into the German society" (Geary 84). As Jews were now declared to be the "Volksfeind" (Aleff 79) number one and Germans were prompted to despise them as their trade partners and friends (Verordnung zur Ausschaltung der Juden aus dem deutschen Wirtschaftsleben 12.11.2938) also put many Germans into an inner conflict because they now had to decide whether to be loyal to their friends or loyal to the state. Through the fact that active propaganda has shown its effect and that the prospect of arrest and torture was omnipresent, the public did denounce fellow citizens (Geary 44). Especially people "harboring dissident opinions in Nazi Germany lived in fear of denunciation, which was often exploited by neighbors, former work mates or even school kids" (Geary 44). Again people in Joanne K. Rowling's novel and people living under Adolf Hitler's rule had to be very careful whom they surround themselves with, as anybody could turn into their enemy.

In conclusion the chapter *Friend or Enemy* has revealed that in both societies the governments have managed to infiltrate into friendships and families, causing people to face each other with mistrust and skepticism. Moreover it has shown in how far people were influenced and changed through effective propaganda, systematic oppression and constant monitoring and that even family ties could be torn apart because of it.

4.4 Voldemort's Death Eaters in Comparison to Adolf Hitler's Schutzstaffel as Executive

Although Lord Voldemort and Adolf Hitler came to power very differently, they nevertheless shared a very important common feature: faithful followers who shared their belief of belonging to a superior group, destined to subjugate and to control others. Moreover they were all convinced that their actions, no matter how cruel and inhumane, were only done for the

35

'greater good', the welfare of the state (Hitler 316; Rowling Hallows 294). With Voldemort's Death Eaters, his "elite force" (Wikia) that he had used already in the First Wizarding War, and Hitler's *Schutzstaffel* (SS), both rulers had created an executive that on the one hand served them for their own personal protection and on the other hand ensured that everyone and everything was running in structured courses. But as the following comparison will show, they had even more in common.

First and most importantly, both executives consisted of people who were selected under the strict criteria of racial biology and belief and stood under the direct command of their Führer (Hofer 79; wikia). This gets underlined by the fact that the Death Eaters closest to Voldemort, such as Bellatrix Lestrange, the Malfoys and the Carrow siblings were all Purebloods and shared the belief that only those "whose ancestry is purest" (Rowling Order 185) have the right to live and rule. Also Adolf Hitler's Schutzstaffel consisted only of members whose ancestry was examined very closely (dhm) and who would do anything in their might to translate Hitler's "völlig unhaltbaren Rassenideen" (Hofer 79) into action. Because of these beliefs both executives played a "disproportionate part in the implementation of the politics of genocide" (Geary 71), as the SS took command of the concentration camps and also the Death Eaters were responsible for the attacks of "large numbers of Muggles" (wikia). From their cruel and brutal actions against the "minderwertige[n] Rassen" (Hofer 80), one can conclude that Voldemort's Death Eaters and Hitler's SS both were responsible for the most terrible crimes against humankind. What happened to people that were tortured by Death Eaters can be observed in the case of Neville Longbottom's parents, who were Aurors that fought against the Dark Lord and who were "tortured to insanity by You-Know-Who's followers" (Rowling Order 454). Here again one can draw a connection to Jews and members of the opposition who have been "eingesperrt, mißhandelt und zu Tode gefoltert" (Hofer 79) by members of the Schutzstaffel. Additionally the expression that people were 'tortured to insanity' hints at the medical experiments made in the concentrations camps which often times lead to a painful death (Hofer 79). Therefore the Death Eaters and the Schutzstaffel also served their rulers for spreading fear and for keeping the crowds under control, because as their proceedings against Jews and members of the opposition show, revolt often had fatal consequences.

Secondly, the aspect of loyalty played a major role for Death Eaters as well as for SS-men who swore eternal allegiance to their masters, as "der allgemeine Leitspruch der SS 'Meine Ehre heißt Treue'" (Nitzschmann 117) proves. In the *Harry Potter* novels the aspect of eternal allegiance is also highly emphasized because being a Death Eater is said to be "a lifetime of service or death" (Rowling Order 104) meaning that either you fulfill the wants and needs of your Master or you will be killed. Nevertheless one has to note here that many followers of the Dark Lord, such as Peter Pettygrew, only showed so much devotion to him through fear. That people and his followers were so afraid of Lord Voldemort that they did not dare to say his name, but instead devotedly called him "Master" (Rowling Order 717) when addressing him directly, or generally "You-know-who" or "He-who-must-not-be-named" can be a hint for that. But also the fact that Bellatrix Lestrange asked Voldemort not to punish her and flung "herself down at Voldemort's feet", right after she had failed to bring him the Prophecy he wanted (Rowling Order 176-7) emphasizes this. Also in the *Third Reich* this phenomenon could be observed as many people joined groups like the Hitler Youth, the League of German Maidens or the SS because not doing so "could be dangerous" (Geary 41). Nevertheless, the SS and the Death Eaters became the most important instrument of power as they had the "full might of the Ministry on their side" (Rowling Hallows 170) to ensure compliance of the new laws. The actions of Death Eaters and SS-men ran completely "outside the control of the police and the judiciary" (Geary 42), reflecting the arbitrariness of their actions and again underlining the unpredictability of the State and its people.

Similarly to members of the SS who infiltrated "Massenorganisationen, wie [die] 'Deutsche Arbeitsfront, [die] 'Hitlerjugend', [die] Studenten-und Dozentenschaft der Hochschulen" (Hofer 79), also Voldemort's Death Eaters have taken over the *Daily Prophet* or have become teachers in order to spread racist ideas (Rowling Hallows 171; 462). The population consequently could not escape the exertion of influence from racist ideas and propaganda.

Another similarity between the two executives can be found in their outward appearances, because with their black uniforms, black coats and belts they stood out from all other people (Appendix 1;2). Furthermore the Schutzstaffel and the Death Eaters were both known as "unheimliche Gestalten in schwarzer Uniform" (Hofer 79). Also the fact that the Death Eaters closest to Lord Voldemort carried a Death Heads tattoo, known as the 'Dark Mark', which he only has to touch and his followers gather around him, can be associated with the *Totenkopfverbänden* of the SS who wore the *Totenkopf* as their emblem on their Uniforms to highlight their difference from other groups. As one can see in the pictures in the appendix, both signs show a significant resemblance and served as identification feature.

All in all one can note that aside from belief and origin, Hitler's Schutzstaffel and Voldemort's Death Eaters shared the characteristics of loyalty, outward appearance and devotion to their Führer or Master. Additionally their proceedings with Jews and non-purebloods or Muggles can be compared as they consisted of great atrocities such as the systematic extermination and abuse of minorities.

4.5 Resistance Groups and Underground Movements

Despite of all efforts to suppress opposition and revolt against the totalitarian system of government by establishing a control apparatus and enacting new laws, people in *Harry Potter* and in the *Third Reich* have nevertheless managed to form resistance groups in order to fight against this system. In the following chapter I will therefore introduce the *Order of the Phoenix* and *Dumbledore's Army* as two institutions that built the resistance groups in Joanne K. Rowling's *Harry Potter and the Order of the Phoenix* and oppose them to the resistance groups formed in Germany during the rule of Adolf Hitler. Furthermore it will be pointed out which features and properties made the resistance in *Harry Potter* so successful.

The first resistance group one gets to know in Joanne K. Rowling's *Harry Potter and the Order of the Phoenix* is of the same name and a "secret society", founded by Albus Dumbledore during the First Wizarding War (Rowling Order 65). Back then "the Order worked with the Ministry to oppose the Dark Lord and his followers" (wikia) and now that nobody would believe them that a Second Wizarding War was about to break out, their task was to convince and recruit people that would fight with them (Rowling Order 88). Using Sirius Blacks' parental home, which was magically hidden between two other houses and which only "inflated, pushing those on either side out of its way" (Rowling Order 58) when someone was memorizing a note written by the founder of *the Order*, as a Headquarter, the members of *the Order* were not only recruiting new members but also trying to protect Muggles and Muggle-borns from being harmed by Death Eaters (Rowling Order 65). The way the Headquarter of *the* Order of the Phoenix was hidden might already evoke the pictures of secret rooms in which Germans have hidden Jewish friends from being captured by Nazis (Kulke). Also the aspect of absolute secrecy was of greatest importance so their doings were not uncovered. Harry for example was not allowed to mention *the Order of the Phoenix* in public for fear of being overheard (Rowling Order 58). Furthermore it is important to mention that every member of *the Order* was risking his job by trying to recruit people, spying in the Ministry of Magic or feeding the Ministry with wrong information (Rowling Order 90). Nevertheless, they all placed the common good above their own, because they realized that: "there's things more importan' than keepin' a job [sic]" (Rowling Order 533) and also that "there are things worth dying for" (Rowling Order 421). Risking ones lives for the lives of others out of conviction that everyone is created equal made the members of *the Order of the Phoenix* not only show moral courage, it also made them heroes. Being active in underground movements was consequently dangerous as it could lead to loosing your job, arrest or even death. Nevertheless one can draw the next connection to the actions taken by members of the opposition in the *Third Reich*, where friends and neighbors of Jews gave shelter to the despised in order to protect them and risked everything for them. Also for those "stille Helden", as people who protected Jews were called, "Schweigen war die oberste Regel" (Kulke). As pointed out in chapter 4.3 the "public willingness to denounce fellow citizens" (Geary 44) was high in the *Third Reich* and as a consequence success and failure of rescue attempts depended highly on the ability to keep silent and to not attract any attention. Although in the *Third Reich* organized groups did not make these acts of protection, but rather individuals, the proceedings were nevertheless similar to those of *the Order of the Phoenix,* as they had to follow the same rules of secrecy to help outsiders because otherwise their efforts could have terrible consequences for themselves as well.

The second resistance group formed in *Harry Potter and the Order of the Phoenix* is a students' resistance group called *Dumbledore's Army,* which was founded by Harry, Hermione and Ron in order to teach students defense against the Dark Arts so they would be prepared to fight against Lord Voldemort and his Death Eaters (Rowling Order 303). But defense against the Dark Arts was not their only aim. Additionally they all wanted to be able to protect themselves. For their own protection they practiced mainly the patronus charm, which serves as a shield against curses and protects positive feelings. Only Harry was taught an additional technique to protect himself. As he was the only one whose mind was also infiltrated by the Dark Lord, who made him see images of true happenings but also manipulated images that brought Harry and his friends in great dangers, Harry had to learn Occlumency: "The magical defense of the mind against external penetration" (Rowling Order 458). In his lessons with Professor Snape he was supposed to learn how to "seal the mind against magical intrusion and influence" (Rowling Order 468) because Voldemort has made use of Harry's brain and even implanted feelings of hate against Dumbledore in Harry. During the lessons the reader also learns that "the key to defending yourself lies not in yelling or shouting, but in using your brain and keeping the enemy out of your thoughts, or more precisely not letting the enemy poison your brain with his views (Rowling Order 472). Also this expression can be compared to the sayings that Germans were infected by the extreme right wing and racist views, and poisoned "von fanatischem Judenhass" (Aleff 80). Through active propaganda, the Nazis have managed to influence and shape society according to their racist needs and beliefs that one can also conclude that they have managed to infiltrate the brains of society. By telling Harry: "Repel me with your brain and you will not need to resort to your wand" (Rowling Order 472), Severus Snape gives him an alternative to fighting someone with weapons because as this quotation and the previous ones show, not letting the enemy into the brain and mind in the first place can serve as prevention since one is no longer vulnerable to mental attacks.

The fact that students come together and fight against the system shows in general that "Totalitarismus bekämpft werden muss" (Nitzschmann121)". And also in the *Third Reich* a student resistance group from Munich, known as the White Rose group became popular for their actions against the regime (Geary 68). Although they did not prepare themselves for a physical combat against the system, they nevertheless

41

handed out leaflets in which they politically enlightened the German people and therefore called on people to passive, and later even to active resistance (Schulz). In their view, the Youth should stand up for themselves and unite against their oppressors because otherwise the German name would be dishonored forever (Schultz). Therefore they fulfilled the same functions as the *Order of the Phoenix* and *Dumbledore's Army* in Joanne K. Rowling's novels. The fact that all members of the *White Rose* group were executed for spreading their enlightening leaflets, shows how dangerous their attempts were and that people gave their lives for their believes. Additionally the labeling of persons who helped to defeat the Dark Lord or Adolf Hitler were very similar, as they were called "blood traitor[s]" (Rowling Order 74) in *Harry Potter* and either "Vaterlandsverräter" or "Nestbeschmutzer" (Rabitz) in the *Third Reich*.

Besides learning how to protect and defend themselves against corporal and mental assaults, the students in *Dumbledore's Army* furthermore learned that friendship, group cohesion and loyalty are key aspects to successfully defend enemies. The fact that "the five wands of Ron, Hermione, Neville, Ginny and Luna rose on either side of him" (Rowling Order 690) when Harry was attacked by Death Eaters in the Ministry of Magic emphasizes this as it shows that only when they are united they are strong. The quotation by Albus Dumbledore who says that: "We can fight it only by showing an equally strong bond of friendship and trust" underlines the fact that if people "stand together [and are] united" (Rowling Order 201; 202) they are more powerful and more likely to succeed as if they were fighting alone. The following example of the Weasley twins serves as proof for this assumption because after Fred and George have openly and under the eyes of all Hogwarts pupils revolted against Umbridge's leadership as they "turned a school corridor into a swamp" (Rowling Order 594), they activated more actions against the new school system. Pupils from now on joined together, turned Umbridge's classes into a complete disaster and invented "Umbridgitis", a disease that made students faint or develop "dangerous fevers" (Rowling Order 597). Also on the corridors, students revolted– and because it was so many of them, even Mr. Filch, the caretaker and admirer of Dolores Umbridge, could not harm them with his whip (Rowling Order 597). Even teachers, who favored Dumbledore and who detested Umbridge as much as the students, started to encourage the student's revolution and supported them (Rowling Order 598). All just for one purpose: to cause so much trouble for Umbridge that the Ministry notices and as a consequence removes her from office because she is not able to handle the situation appropriately. Here we can see, that the revolution against the system is finally starting to pay off, as more and more pupils join in. Whereas at first it has only been about two hands full of pupils, that could not accomplish very much, it was now almost the whole school that was demonstrating and actually succeeding.

To conclude the findings of this chapter one can say that despite all the restrictions by the government, resistance groups such as the White Rose group in the *Third Reich* and the *Order of the Phoenix* and *Dumbledore's Army* in *Harry Potter* have nevertheless succeeded to organize themselves and started to revolt against the oppressive system. Although the realization of their efforts differed, the *White Rose* group and the resistance groups in *Harry Potter* still shared the same goals: to enlighten people about the government's true plans, to raise awareness of the misanthropic happenings in society and to form a larger resistance group. In order to achieve their goals both groups had to act in the underground, trying to keep their doings as secret as possible because they were not only risking their jobs but even their lives.

5. Conclusion

In conclusion, analyzing Joanne K. Rowling's fantasy novel *Harry Potter and the Order of the Phoenix* against the background of the happenings in the *Third Reich* has shown that in the novel many aspects of history and reality have been connected with fantasy. More precisely the paper has presented that in Joanne K. Rowling's novel one could detect similarities between the understandings of race and how supposedly 'inferior' people should be treated in the fictional world of *Harry Potter* and in the *Third Reich*. Similarly to Hitler, Lord Voldemort distinguished between different 'races' based on pseudo-scientific definitions of race and came to the conclusion that all people of 'non-pure blood' threatened the welfare of society and should therefore be eradicated. In the *Third Reich* and in the fantasy novel a so-called 'true blood agenda' was set into being that should 'clean' the 'royal' blood of Aryans and Purebloods from the 'poisonous' blood of 'filthy' Jews and Mudbloods. Moreover the second part of this paper has displayed that for the fear of being overthrown by oppositional groups and in order to strengthen their power, both governments have established a totalitarian state in which every aspect of the society member's lives was under their surveillance and their control. By controlling the media, enacting new laws and threatening them with severe punishments and even death, both rulers suppressed their citizens and limited them in their freedom of speech and freedom of action.

Furthermore the final chapter has presented that also the resistance groups have shown great similarities, because the White Rose group, the *Order of the Phoenix* and *Dumbledore's Army* wanted to enlighten society about the injustices that were taking place and encourage people to passively and actively revolt against the inhumane and brutal regime. Nevertheless the fact that the members of the *White Rose* group were all executed whereas *Dumbledore's Army* and the *Order of the Phoenix* only had very few losses shows that one could also find differences between the happenings in the *Third Reich* and in *Harry Potter*. Moreover the fact

44

that Joanne K. Rowling puts so much emphasis on the values of friendship, loyalty, solidarity and group cohesion reflects that to her these were the key values that made revolt in *Harry Potter and the Order of the Phoenix* so successful. At this point one might on the one hand argue that she emphasized the importance of these values and created this happy ending because she wanted to fulfill the moral aspect of children's books and show people how to defend an enemy successfully and on the other hand one might say that especially here the fictional aspect becomes most evident because in real life there is not always an happy end.

All in all the findings of this paper have shown that a culturally and historically educated reader who takes a more critical look at this fantasy novel could detect many connections between happenings in 'real life' and the life presented in the novels. Fantasy novels consequently do offer an insight to culture and sociology, leaving it to the reader to find and comment on these parallels.

6. Works Cited

Primary Literature

Hitler, Adolf. *Mein Kampf.* Zwei Bände in einem Band. Ungekürzte Ausgabe. München: Zentralverlag der NSDAP., Frz. Eher Nachf., G.m.b.H. 1943. Print.

Rowling, Joanne K. *Harry Potter and the Deathly Hallows.* Great Britain: Bloomsburry publishing Plc: 2007. Print.

Rowling, Joanne K. *Harry Potter and the Order of the Phoenix.* Great Britain: Bloomsburry publishing Plc London. 2003. Print.

Secondary Literature

Aleff, Eberhard: *Edition Zeitgeschehen: Das Dritte Reich.* Hannover: Fackelträger-Verlag. 1970. Print.

Bimberg, C.: *The Place of Children's Literature Studies in English and American Studies in Germany: Empowering the Young Generation to 'See Through'.* Proceedings Anglistentag 2000 Berlin. Ed. Peter Lucko and Jürgen Schläger. Trier: Wissenschaftlicher Verlag. 2001. Print.

Erdheim, M: *Revolution, Totem und Tabu. Vom Verenden der Revolution im Wiederholungszwang. Ethnopsychoanalyse2. Herrschaft, Anpassung, Widerstand.* Frankfurt am Main: 1991. Print.

Geary, Dick: *Hitler and Nazism.* Second Edition. New York: Routledge. 2000. Print.

Giesecke, Hermann. *Hitlers Pädagogen. Theorie und Praxis nationalsozialistischer Erziehung.* Weinheim, München: Juventa Verlag Weinheim und München. 1993. Print.

Grenby, M.O: „Fantasy". *Children's Literature.* Edinburgh: Edinburgh University Press. 2008. Print.

Hildebrand, Klaus. *Oldenbourg Grundriss der Geschichte: Das dritte Reich.* München: R. Oldenbourg Verlag GmbH. 1987. Print.

Himmler, Heinrich: *Die Schutzstaffel als antibolschewistische Kampforganisation*. München. 1936.

Hofer, Walther: *Der Nationalsozialismus. Dokumente 1922-1945*. Frankfurt am Main: Fischer Taschenbuch GmbH.1957. Print.

Hunt, Peter: *An Introduction to Children's Literature*. Oxford: Oxford University Press.1994. Print.

Jellinek, L.: *Das Phänomen Harry Potter. Eine literaturwissenschaftliche Analyse des Welterfolgs*. VDM Verlag. 2006. Print.

Jensen, Jeff: *„Fire Storm"*. Entertainment Weekly. September 7th 2000. http://www.accio-quote.org/articles/2000/0900-ew-jensen.htm (access date: 31.03.2014)

Kershaw, Ian. *The Nazi Dictatorship: Problems and Perspectives of Interpretation*. London: Ltd. 1985. Print.

Kielinger, T.: *Potters wahres Ich*. Die Welt, 26.02.2007:8

Krekeler, E.: *Jugend im Widerstand*. DIE WELT, 09.07.2007

Kulke Ulli: *Wo und wie 1700 Juden die Nazis überlebten*. Die Welt. 15.09.2009. http://www.welt.de/kultur/article4525767/Wo-und-wie-1700-Juden-die-Nazis-ueberlebten.html (access date: 04.04.2014)

Kühn, Heike: *Liebe zum beunruhigenden Detail. Weil Harry und die Seinen den Kinderschuhen entwachsen sind, geht es diesmal gruseliger zu*. FR, 17.11.2005

Lesnik-Oberstein, Karln: *Children's Literature. Criticism and the fictional child*. Oxford: Clarendon Press. 1994. Print.

Manlove, Colin: *The Fantasy Literature of England*. Basingstoke: Macmillan. New York: St. Martin's Press. 1999. Print

Michalka, Wolfgang: *Das Dritte Reich*, Bd. 1. München: Deutscher Taschenbuch Verlag. 1985. Print.

Mosse, George L. *Der nationalsozialistische Alltag. So lebte man unter Hitler*. Königstein/Ts: Athenäum Verlag GmbH. 1978. Print.

Nitzschmann, Karin: *Die phantastische Welt des Harry Potter.* Analyse des siebenbändigen Entwicklungsromans. Frankfurt am Main: Brandes & Apsel. 2007. Print.

Nürnberger Gesetze

Potjans, Mareike: Der Nürnberger Prozess. Planet Wissen. 04.02.2014 http://www.planet-wissen.de/politik_geschichte/nachkriegszeit/stunde_null/nuernberge r_prozess.jsp (access date: 05.03.2014)

Rabitz, Cornelia: *Stille Helden- Hilfe für verfolgte Juden.* Dw. 09.05.2012. http://www.dw.de/stille-helden-hilfe-für-verfolgte-juden/a-15938210. (access date: 04.04.2014)

"Race". Collier's Encyclopedia. 1969 ed. Print.

"Race". Encyclopaedia Britannica. 1994 ed. Print.

"Race". The Cambridge Encyclopedia. 1997 ed. Print.

Rauschning, Hermann: Gespräche mit Hitler. Zürich/New York: Europa Verlag. 1940. Print.

Reichsgesetzblatt Jg. 1933, Teil 1, Nr. 17

Reichsgesetzblatt Jg. 1933, Teil 1, Nr. 111

Reichsgesetzblatt Jg. 1936, Teil 1, Nr. 113

Schulz, Kirsten. *Studentischer Widerstand: „Die Weiße Rose".* Bundeszentrale für politische Bildung. 20.04.2005. http://www.bpb.de/geschichte/nationalsozialismus/weisse-rose/60945/studentischer-widerstand (access date: 22.03.2014)

Sullivan, C.W.: „High Fantasy." *International Companion Encyclopedia of Children's Literature.* Ed. Peter Hunt, London and New York: Routledge. 1996. Print.

Unknown Author: *Death Eaters.* Harry Potter Wiki. http://harrypotter.wikia.com/wiki/Death_Eaters (access date: 01.04.2014)

Unknown Author: *Die Schutzstaffel (SS)*. Deutsches historisches Museum.
https://www.dhm.de/lemo/html/nazi/innenpolitik/ss/ (access date: 02.04.2014)

Unknown Author: *Order of the Phoenix*. Harry Potter Wiki.
http://harrypotter.wikia.com/wiki/Order_of_the_Phoenix (access date: 01.04.2014)

Unknown Author: „*Pottermania"– 450 Millionen in 15 Jahren*. DIE WELT, 26.06.2012
http://www.welt.de/kultur/literarischewelt/article107271656/Potterma nia-450-Millionen-Buecher-in-15-Jahren.html (access date: 28.02 2014)

Unknown Author: *The Nuremberg Laws: Background and Overview*.
Jewish Virtual Library.
http://www.jewishvirtuallibrary.org/jsource/Holocaust/nurlaws.html (access date: 10.03.2014)

Zimmermann, Karl: *Das Dritte Reich. Bausteine zum neuen Staat und Volk. Die geistigen Grundlagen des Nationalsozialismus*. Leipzig. Quelle& Meyer Verlag. 1933. Print.

7. Appendix

1. Lord Voldemort and his Death Eaters

http://img2.wikia.nocookie.net/__cb20110418214318/harrypotter/images/c/c4/DH_2_Death_Eaters_with_Voldemort_during_the_battle.jpg

2. Members of the SS Division Totenkopf

Bundesarchiv Bild 192-206, KZ Mauthausen, SS-Männer vor Gefangenen.jpg

3.   Death   Heads   Sign   of   the   SS   Division   Totenkopf

4. Kragenspiegel that was sewn to the Collar of the Division Totenkopfs Uniforms

http://www.hermann-historica.de/auktion/images63_max/18733.jpg

4. The Dark Mark

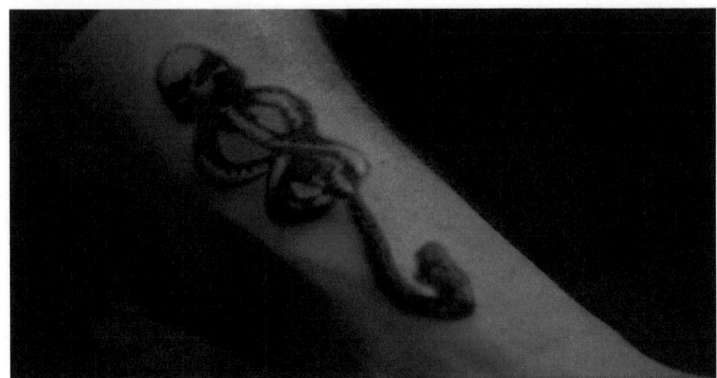

http://img1.wikia.nocookie.net/__cb20090814005331/harrypotter/images/e/
e3/DarkMarkCrouch.JPG